True
Friends

A REVOLUTIONARY APPROACH
TO CULTIVATING CONSCIOUS
FEMININE FRIENDSHIPS

ROCHONDA
FERRELLI

True Friends: A Revolutionary Approach to Cultivating
Conscious Feminine Friendships

Published by Rochonda Ferrelli

Copyright © 2022 Rochonda Ferrelli

Hardcopy ISBN: 979-8-88831-047-2
E-book ISBN: 979-8-88831-048-9

DEDICATION

I dedicate this book to my teachers, Jim Dethmer and Diana Chapman, cofounders of the Conscious Leadership Group. Thank you for inspiring a newfound presence in my life from which this work flows, and for doing all that you do.

And to all of my friends, past, present, and future, thank you for the experience of knowing you and for being a part of my journey.

With love, Ro

Free Bonuses
Gifts From the Author

I hope you enjoy the true stories and transformational exercises shared in this book. It's my intention that you absorb this information and that it evolves who you are on a deep level.

I've created 2 free trainings and a handful of resources to support your journey to creating true friendships in your life. You can access them by visiting this website:

www.RochondaFerrelli.com/TrueFriends

Cheers to true friendship and the evolution of women.

Table of Contents

INTRODUCTION

My Best-Friend Illusion

I distinctly remember having a strong desire for lifelong friendships when I was about 14. I'm not exactly sure if this desire came about because my mom and I had been moving around from home to home after her divorce from my stepdad, which made it really hard for me to stay in touch with friends, or if it stemmed from being raised as an only child. Or if it was just a part of a bigger plan that the Universe has had all this time.

Most likely it was a combination of these.

My friendships have always meant so much more to me than "just friends"—because I treat them with a reverence that's more like family. But at the same time, I've struggled with them.

In junior high, I attended three schools in a two-year period. And then finally, my mom and I moved in with my grandparents in Independence, Missouri, so that I could do all four years at one high school. This gave us both some stability while my mom picked up her life after a traumatic divorce, and I did my best to survive the cringeworthy teenage years.

One friend in particular, Amanda, and I met in one of the junior high schools I went to, then we got to reconnect when we both ended up attending the same high school. When I started high school that fall, it was such a relief to have at least one friend I knew from before. While my world sucked in so many ways—you know, with another new school, acne, starting fresh again with no friends, typical teenage insecurities, and now living with my grandparents—knowing I had one friend in school to look forward to was such a gift.

Amanda was into modeling, art, and hip-hop. She had a very unique fashion sense. Not to mention she was beautiful. We had so much fun together practicing our dance moves, rapping, memorizing the latest Eminem song lyrics (which we wrote out by hand word for word), smoking cigarettes and other things, enjoying White Castle cheeseburgers with pineapple soda from the Save A Lot grocery store, and, of course, getting caught up in boyfriend drama.

After we graduated, we both soul-searched and ended up moving away from our hometown. She moved to New York City to pursue modeling, and I moved to South Beach, Florida, to start a new life near the ocean.

Shortly after my move, it hit me that I knew no one and was living by myself in a small one-bedroom apartment a few blocks from the Atlantic Ocean. It was bittersweet. There I was, starting a new life in a beautiful new place, but it was also lonely. South Beach is small, and most people there are tourists and seasonal snowbirds. So, making new friends wasn't as easy as I'd expected.

In my loneliness, I noticed for the first time just how one-sided my relationship with Amanda actually was. A few years earlier, my grandmother had pointed this out to me, sharing that she felt Amanda wasn't there for me like I was there for her. But hearing this enraged me. I got defensive and stood up for my friend, insisting that my grandmother didn't know what she was talking about. Sadly, at that time I couldn't see what she was seeing, and that was the last time it was brought up.

A month after my move to Florida, I found out that Amanda would be in South Beach to model during the high season for fashion week. I was thrilled and looked forward to seeing my longtime best friend.

The day her plane landed, I was ready and available to pick her up from the airport and soooo excited to see her, show her my new apartment, and catch up on everything.

She assured me she didn't need a ride, since her modeling agency had already arranged one for her and the girls she was traveling with.

"Okay, cool! So I'll see you after you get in then!" I said. But the day passed, and it got late, and there was no sign of her.

I worked over the next couple of days. Amanda and I spoke briefly while playing phone tag, and she indicated that she wasn't sure when we'd get to see each other. She said she didn't have a schedule and just had to be ready to go to work at any moment.

After a few weeks of going back and forth, I realized that seeing each other wasn't as much of a priority to her as it was to me.

If you've ever been to South Beach, then you know it's a very small island around nine miles long. And Amanda was literally staying three blocks from my apartment. Disappointment and frustration sank in. After a month, I couldn't believe we'd been only three blocks away from each other for the past month and she still wasn't able to make a quick visit. Not even 15 minutes or a short breakfast!

We finally did get to meet up for a night out with her new modeling friends, whom I enjoyed. Amanda and I always did have a great time together. So I tucked away the disappointment and anger that I'd been feeling and moved on.

Later in that trip she expressed how broke she was. As in no-money broke because the modeling work she was doing hadn't paid her yet. I too was broke, having spent all of my savings just to get into my apartment. After paying first and last month's rent, plus deposit, I had $225 to my name to pay bills and eat. Without thinking, I went to the bank and withdrew $100 to give her. I placed it in an envelope with a note. It was literally breaking me to do this, but I knew I'd get a paycheck soon and would somehow figure it out. I thought, *She's my best friend, and I'd do anything for her.* I wasn't sure if she'd accept the money, so I planned to slide it under her apartment door as an anonymous gift. But for some reason, something in me said to hold on to the envelope and not give it to her just yet.

We hung out a few more times while she was in town. We went to some amazing parties on Star Island at millionaires' mansions, got into some of the best nightclubs on South Beach because of her modeling agency's connections, and had the time of our lives. We were broke, but we were young and beautiful— and hey, we were in South Beach living the dream, baby!

Toward the end of her visit, I had a feeling in my gut. The feeling said I needed that money I was planning to give her. It was all I had to survive on. And a sad realization sank in: she probably wouldn't have done the same for me. So I kept it and never mentioned it to her. And we moved on.

But I still considered her my best friend.

I visited Amanda in New York City one time. She was renting a room the size of my bathroom in a tiny apartment, which she paid astronomically high rent for. If you've ever been to New York City, you know what I'm talking about.

But it didn't bother me. I was there to see her and have fun, and that was all that mattered! And we did have fun. We went to underground nightclubs, met up with boys, and danced to music that I'd never heard before. It was a different vibe from my South Florida life. And to be honest with you, I wasn't crazy about it. New York is a concrete jungle compared to the lush and vibrant South Florida views I'd come to love. It also just felt overwhelming with so many people to see and places to go.

Also, I could feel a shift in Amanda as she settled into the person she was meant to be. I accepted it, but at the same time, I couldn't deny the space forming between us.

Looking back with what I know now, I can see this was an opportunity for mourning. Sometimes, when people change or move away, it's an opportunity for us to mourn the loss and the way things used to be.

But that's not what I did. I gripped on tight to what was, and I kept my sadness, disappointment, and anger tucked away deep inside. This led to feelings of resentment, which always ends up snowballing. I'll show you what I'm talking about.

Amanda sometimes traveled to Miami for modeling jobs. Her friend Sam, a wealthy and older bachelor who was generous with his money, would sometimes pay for her flights and give her a place to stay on South Beach. Sometimes she visited me on those trips, and sometimes she would literally be a thirty-minute drive away and I wouldn't find out she'd been in Florida until she was already back home. *What the actual fuck? Isn't she my best friend? If I was that close to her, I'd always make an effort to stop by and see her*, I thought.

A few years after meeting my husband, we began planning our wedding. He wanted a big wedding, but I wanted to save that money and put it toward a new home. We finally agreed to have a big wedding. When we told our friends and family about those plans, the burden and stress of wedding planning sank in. So we changed our minds and decided on a whim to leave for Las Vegas, giving everyone only two weeks' notice. Whoever could come, would come. And whoever couldn't make it, we would understand.

I knew it was a last-minute request, but even so, I was still really counting on having at least one friend at my wedding. But no friends could make it. I was desperate and asked Amanda twice. There was nothing she could do, as she had an important and high-paying modeling job scheduled for the day of the wedding. I understood. But I was still upset and did my best to not let it show. I also felt ashamed that I had no friends who were willing to drop their plans and meet me in Vegas for my special day.

Look, I get it. The modeling industry isn't easy. And when you land a good job, it's likely paying bills that you've been stressing over since your last gig. So I do understand why she couldn't make it. But at the same time, I thought, *I'd do ANYTHING for my best friend. Anything in the world. I'd drop whatever it was to be there for her. No questions.*

I had no right to hold this grudge against her, but hold it I did. I couldn't help it. My wedding was a once-in-a-lifetime experience, and she wasn't there for me when I needed her the most.

And not only that, she didn't even try to fly out the next few days to celebrate with us in Vegas or to visit the next week, or even the next month. There was no attempt at resolution.

Again, the disappointment and anger sank into my chest. And my snowball of anger, disappointment, and resentment continued to build.

When Amanda's father died, it was unexpected and heartbreaking. I knew her dad. I grew up staying at his house and passing through his car dealership parking lot as Amanda and I walked to boys' houses and hit up the local Save A Lot grocery store for snacks.

I immediately looked up flights to meet her in Missouri. I didn't have the extra money to travel. In fact, I was flat broke from honeymooning in Ireland. But I figured I'd just put it on a credit card. After all, this was the death of her father, and I wanted to be there for her.

But after we spoke on the phone, she discouraged me from coming. I still wanted to go, though. I wanted to fly in and show my love and support in this way. But after our phone call, I reflected on all the times she hadn't been there for me when I needed her, and I decided not to attend. I felt sad because I did want to be there. But I knew she wouldn't have done the same for me. So I left it alone and followed up with her a couple of days after the service.

After marriage comes the baby in the baby carriage, and the year after my wedding, I was now pregnant with my daughter. Traditionally, a best friend helps with the baby shower by sending invitations, picking the decor/theme, setting up and breaking down the party, and taking note of the gifts so proper thank-yous can be sent.

But there was no sign of Amanda stepping up to help in this way.

Back in my hometown in Missouri, my mom graciously planned a shower that family and friends could attend. It was a beautiful and successful event that I was so grateful for. Amanda did coordinate her visit home so that she could come to my baby shower, but she didn't offer to help in any way. I asked her for help, and I was counting on it, but she had scheduled all of her doctor appointments during her visit, which left no time for anything else while she was there. She came to the party, we enjoyed each other's company, and then she left.

My snowball of anger, disappointment, and resentment continued building.

My daughter was a year old by now, and a lot of time had passed since Amanda and I had seen each other. I wanted to visit her in New York City, but when I reached out to make the plans, she suggested I get my own hotel room because she didn't have the space for visitors in her new place. I was thinking, *I'd sleep on the floor. We could put a yoga mat down. It's only for one or two nights.* I thought of all the times distant family had visited my grandparents over the years and how, even when there wasn't room, we made room. Amanda wasn't making room for me, and I took offense.

Hotel prices were astronomical, so I decided not to go.

When my daughter was two, I invested in a writer's workshop that happened to be in New York City. I thought of telling Amanda I'd be there and making dinner plans one night to catch up. And then I thought of all the times she hadn't been there for me as I'd hoped she'd be, the times she'd visited Miami and I didn't know she was there, how she hadn't come to (or even celebrated) my wedding, how she hadn't been fully engaged to help out at my baby shower, and the times I'd attempted to visit but couldn't stay with her. And so I decided, for the first time, that I needed to move on with my life like she was moving on with hers.

I went to New York City and enjoyed the conference. And the next time we caught up on the phone, I casually mentioned it. She was shocked that I'd been so close to her and hadn't reached out. I played it just like she had, saying, "Yeah, there wasn't any free time, really. I was only there for four days. Such a busy schedule. We'll catch each other next time."

The last straw was when Amanda got married. My daughter was three now, and she didn't know Amanda like I'd hoped she would.

Like me, Amanda decided to get married on a whim, and she did so at her local New York City courthouse. She was able to FaceTime one person during the ceremony using her cell phone—and she chose her childhood friend, Casey, whom she'd known since she was two years old.

I learned about the wedding when Amanda called me a few days after the service to tell me the big news.

But instead of being happy for her, my heart broke. I could barely compose myself as she described the wedding and the rush of events. I knew Casey. The three of us had hung out from time to time. And I always knew Casey would be Amanda's maid of honor, since they'd known each other their whole lives. We'd even talked about it when planning our weddings as teenagers. But it still hurt to know that I wasn't invited and that Amanda didn't consider borrowing another phone to FaceTime two people, or figure out a three-way call, or even call me the morning of or that afternoon.

No. She called me three days later.

And for the first time, I realized that this whole time, although she was my best friend, I wasn't hers.

I felt I wasn't good enough. I felt left out. The anger and disappointment I'd felt before were now an internal rage that boiled in every limb of my body. My sadness was now despair.

I held myself together on that phone call the best I could, holding my breath in between my words when I said, "I'm so, so, so happy for the both of you. It sounds like it was a really nice ceremony. I'm wishing the two of you many years of happiness together."

The words were forced. Robotic. Fake.

I cut the call short. I could barely hold myself together. As soon as I hung up, I sobbed.

A few months later, after writing out my feelings and thoughts and going to therapy, I called Amanda. I was on a visit to our hometown in Missouri. The weather was cold, and I could see my breath as I took the call outside my grandparents' house to speak privately.

My voice shook in unison with my hands. My heart was pounding, and my stomach twisted in knots. I paced the driveway. As hard as it was to have this conversation, I knew I had to speak my truth. There was no way around it. I looked down at my notes that I'd prepared for the call, and dialed her number.

"Amanda, this whole time, you've been my best friend. But I realize now that I haven't been yours," I said. "And I'm sorry for putting you on this pedestal and expecting you to be someone you're not. And then getting angry with you for not meeting my expectations for you as my best friend. I need to move on with my life, though." The conversation concluded with examples of all the times I felt angry but never fully expressed it and held it against her.

That was the last time we spoke. She never tried to call or message me afterward. She didn't put effort into restoring our friendship or apologizing. Her lack of response was validating. And as painful as this was, it was the truth.

We always do the best we know how to do. And while I did my best to take radical responsibility in that clearing conversation—**because I could see how I'd manifested the experience of our uneven friendship from childhood trauma**—I still felt anger and resentment toward her even though I tried not to.

I'm going to dive into exactly what radical responsibility is, and is not, very shortly. But for now, just know that when we take radical responsibility, we're owning our 100% for creating the experience we're having with another person.

The clearing conversation I had with Amanda was powerful in that it revealed to both of us the true nature of the relationship and allowed me to move forward without her in my life. It also gave me the opportunity to feel my feelings and express them—but not fully. And because I still felt some anger, resentment, and blame toward her, my best-friend wound never fully healed. As a result, a negative energetic residue was left over from the breakup that would continue to affect how I energetically showed up in all of my friendships moving forward. I was trying to own my 100%, but I wasn't successful in doing so because at the time, I didn't have all the tools I do today.

I can see now that my unhealthy attachment to our friendship and the fantasy I'd built around it stemmed from not feeling good enough about myself and outsourcing my approval to her instead of giving that approval to myself. I can also see where these feelings originated when I take a deeper look at my childhood traumas around abandonment by my father and then *again* by my stepfather, as well as the range of physical, mental, emotional, and sexual abuse I went through.

In my relationship with Amanda, I hid my feelings of not being good enough beneath overcommitting and over-giving, as well as my insecurity, loneliness, and unhealthy attachment to someone who was clearly just living her life. There's really nothing to blame her for. Amanda was just showing up how she shows up.

The insecure and over-giving part of me, however, required someone in my life who I could be that way with. Amanda was just a character in my life's play. If it hadn't been her playing that role, it would've been another woman playing the part. This is why when we don't fully heal, we continue to attract the same types of people in our lives. The Universe will keep sending these teachers to us disguised as friends until we finally learn the lesson we need to learn once and for all.

Don't kill the messengers. The friends who are triggering you are allies in your personal growth.

CHAPTER 1

Are You Disappointed in and Frustrated with Your Relationships with Women?

If you consistently feel disappointed and frustrated in your relationships with other women, this book will show you that **the decision to take radical responsibility in your life is the key** to creating long-lasting friendships that are genuine, supportive, and deeply fulfilling. When I look back and scan through all the different friendships I've had throughout my life, there are only a couple friends I've known for many years who are still near and dear to my heart. In most cases, friendships dissolved as we drifted apart into life's new chapters. And in other instances, there was an argument that led to a breakup.

Even as I sat down to write this book, I found myself in a couple of friendship shitstorms—one that led to a pause in the relationship and another that sadly led to the friendship's end. So while I'm not always the perfect friend (if that even exists), I am human, and with that comes mistakes, learning, and growth, which I'm honored to share with you here.

Over the past few years, I've paid closer attention to the friends I give my energy to, the women I seem to naturally attract into my life, to why I attract them in the first place, and to the types of friendships I ultimately want to surround myself with. The decluttering process hasn't been easy, but it's some of the best personal-growth work I've done. And while it's been an interesting, insightful, and hard road at times, it's what needed to happen so that I could finally start enjoying more fulfilling relationships.

And the better it gets, the better it gets! I promise.

So, here I am, in my imperfectness, answering the call to explore the topic of female friendships more deeply through writing this book. My intention is to help you see yourself and your relationships through a different lens so that this new perspective can support your journey and bring transformation to your life by guiding you to create true friendships that are deeply fulfilling and meaningful.

However, from all the conversations I've had with other women on this topic, there seems to be a universal agreement that, in general, women can be difficult to get along with.

Why is that?

On one side, women can be the most loving, nurturing, thoughtful, kindhearted givers in the world; and on the other, they can become your worst nightmare in the blink of an eye. You know what I'm talking about. We've all seen women throw each other under the bus, backstab, gossip, and be judgmental, unnecessarily competitive, and just downright nasty to one another.

And I'm willing to bet that **we've all** been on both sides of this drama at one point or another. Now, I can't recall a time when I intentionally backstabbed a friend, but I'm sure somewhere along the way I did so unintentionally. I can recall, however, times when I gossiped, was judgmental, acted like I was superior, or acted just flat-out rude. And if you look deep enough within yourself, I'm sure you can recall moments in your life when you did too.

I'm not proud of this behavior, and I'm sure you're not either.

And then there have been times when we were gossiped about, bullied and belittled, judged for an endless number of things, backstabbed, and insulted. And if you think I'm referring only to high school years here, you're wrong. I'm sad to say that all of these things happen to women even as adults! In fact, these behaviors are handed down to children by their parents. So yes, adult women are behaving this way.

But I don't think any of us woke up one day and said, "I'm going to be a fucking bitch today! I'm going to backstab that Susan so good, she won't know what hit her." Now, maybe you know someone who is vindictive like this, or maybe that was you once upon a time. But in general, I don't think we're going around intentionally hurting other women in this way. We do, however, show up just how we show up. And how we show up is going to be interpreted differently by every single person.

What I mean by this is that we're just living life responding, reacting, and doing the best we know how to do at any given time. The things we say, the attitude we have when we say them, the volume of our voices, how we behave, the actions we take, and even our values and core beliefs are going to be interpreted by others in a million different ways.

And likewise, your perception of others is going to be uniquely filtered and interpreted by you as well. This is because the mind's job is to take in data and interpret it through our own filters and past programming. The filters and programs in our minds are created based on our upbringing, pains, pleasures, likes, dislikes, levels of understanding, interactions with others, beliefs, values, traumas, and essentially all of our life experiences from the womb to this now moment.

Here's an example. If I say, "The future is female!" to a hundred people, I'll get a hundred different responses. One person might agree, give an enthusiastic high five, and say, "Hey girl, you got that right!" Another might question how that's even possible. Perhaps they live in a part of the world where girls aren't encouraged to go to school and women aren't treated equal to men. Someone else might smirk and say, "Who cares?" Another person might be inspired and filled with hope at the thought. And another person might completely be triggered by that statement and respond with a feminist attack.

So you see, we're all interpreting things differently, and there's no getting around this. Every single human's perception is unique and different. No two people are ever having the same experience or perceiving anything the same way. So going back to my point: women are showing up just how they show up. And we're each interpreting everyone and everything in our own unique ways.

When there's an aversion or attraction to another person or something they've said or done, it's important to look at that more closely within yourself to see what part of you wants to be known and better understood. Aversions to others tell us about the parts of ourselves that we haven't yet loved and accepted. Attractions to others let us know what we accept within ourselves and want to experience more of.

Let's look more closely at aversions and the things we find most triggering in our relationships with other women. When another woman has shown up in a way that you dislike, maybe you get angry and blame her for making you feel the way you feel. But you feel how you feel because of the way you're wired, programed, and uniquely interpreting things. She's not making you feel anything. She's just showing up how she shows up in the world. And because of your unique perception of how she's showing up, you get emotionally triggered in response to that. No one makes you feel anything. You are the only one responsible for your feelings.

Our triggers are gold mines. But we often stop our journey here instead of taking the time to go a little deeper.

Don't stop here! There's gold awaiting you. When you take the time to look at your trigger, allow your feelings to surface, and then reflect on what lies beneath, that, my friend, is where you access a golden trove of guiding wisdom unique to you. It's one of the most profound tools I know for leveling up and stepping into your highest potential. And when you do this as a regular practice, an evolution of your state of being occurs naturally.

After surveying hundreds of women, I've found some of the most common reasons we feel frustrated and disappointed in our relationships with one another. This list is not all inclusive, but it's a good foundation. As you go through it, make a mental note of the ones you feel most triggered by in your relationships with other women.

1. Abandonment. One day you're friends, hanging out all the time, and then all of a sudden, you're not. *What the hell? I thought we were friends!* you think as you wonder if you did something wrong. Here's the thing: friendship abandonment happens for many different reasons, and I'll share a few here. For starters, the person who abandons the friendship may not feel that there's anything to gain from being in it. I'll talk more on this in a little bit. Or perhaps you (or she) passed judgment and nothing was ever said about it, which then leads to an energetic disconnect in the relationship. When you don't speak up about things that bother you or you have a judgment toward your friend, you'll naturally take an energetic step back in the relationship. This energetic step back will then manifest as a disconnect in some way. For example, constant misaligned schedules that make it impossible to schedule plans, feelings of being distant even though the other person is nearby or only a phone call away, or an emotional buildup over time that results in a sudden explosion over something small.

2. Competition: Unspoken (and often unconscious) competition is formed against friends when there's jealousy or a mentality of there not being enough to go around. Don't fall for this. A scarcity mentality is a trap. Competition and jealousy are often disguised as anger toward your friend, so make sure to do the deeper work of seeing what lies beneath the surface.

3. Criticism: Criticism happens when a person is insecure, projects their insecurities onto another person, then tears them down, or when they are constantly self-deprecating. We all have an inner critic. The problem comes up when we don't look at our criticisms of others and see how those criticisms are also true for ourselves. I'll talk more on this under "Insecurities" and "Judgments" below.

4. Drama: Drama happens. But it's how you deal with it that matters. And there are just some women who are constantly tangled up in a slew of problems or issues. Excessive drama hijacks the energy of friendships by consuming conversations, plans, and your energy, which may leave you feeling depleted instead of energized. There's a difference between helping out a friend in a time of need and being in a codependent and drama-enabling relationship. Know that difference and pay attention to how you feel after hanging out with a friend.

5. Flakiness: Women who make commitments and then cancel at the very last minute or simply don't show up at all are flaky and inconsiderate of the other person's time. But there's also a HUGE energy breach happening here. An energy breach happens when we're out of integrity. When we're in integrity, we have an energetic wholeness that contributes to a constant energetic flow state in our lives. *Hello, synchronicities and problems that resolve themselves!* The Universe responds to,

24

moves through, and can be more supportive to those who are in a state of energetic wholeness. Yes, things come up—such is life! But are you reaching out to renegotiate the change of plans in a timely and considerate way, or are you being a flake?

6. Gossiping: Talking about another woman in a way that you wouldn't if she were present is gossiping. Gossiping is socially acceptable in every culture around the world. We were raised in families that gossip, and we live in a society where gossiping is very normal and even bonding. Research shows that gossiping led to the evolution of the human language because tribes and small communities wanted to know who could be trusted and who they should watch out for. So I get it—gossiping is a way to communicate and bond for most people. However, it's also incredibly damaging to the person being talked about and says more about you than it does about them. Remember, if a friend gossips to you, they'll also gossip about you. Conscious women don't gossip about others, and they don't participate by listening to others' gossip. Instead, they speak directly to the person they're having an issue with and abort conversations that involve gossiping.

7. Insecurities: Look, we all have insecurities. The problem occurs when your insecurities sabotage your relationships by leading you to feel jealous, envious, or angry toward friends or acquaintances, and you don't do the deeper work of self-discovery that will show you what those feelings want to teach you. We project our insecurities onto others and see faults in them, which leads to arguments, judgments, miscommunications, and made-up stories in our minds about the other person. If you can own your insecurities and reveal them to your friend instead of projecting them on her, the insecurity loses its power over you. The vulnerability of your share will bring the right friends—your true friends—even closer to you through this authentic connection. And not to mention all the learning you gain in your personal-growth journey that's irreplaceable and deeply transformative. Eating your judgments instead of projecting them onto others is how you build confidence, accept your imperfections, develop empathy toward others, source approval of yourself from within, and grow as a woman by becoming a true friend yourself.

8. Jealousy: This is one of the more prominent and destructive behaviors between women. The problem with jealousy is that often we don't even realize when we're feeling and behaving this way. It's an unconscious behavior that disguises itself in a myriad of ways by showing up as attention-seeking, anger, disappointment, judgment, disgust, and the need to make yourself feel better than others. It's a behavior that we're all at fault for feeling and acting out on at some point. The trick is to look at any repeating toxic relationships and ask yourself, "Am I jealous at all? What is my jealousy pointing to?" Then, once you know what you're jealous about, you'll be able to redirect yourself to work on accepting these aspects of yourself and your life. Jealousy is pointing to the things that we want for ourselves and is a powerful guidance tool, showing us what we want when leveraged properly.

9. Judgments: Our brains are constantly judging others, and this can be troublesome when you don't fully understand what Carl Jung pointed out: "We do not see others as they are, we only see them as we are." Our judgments of others are mirrors of our own unconscious behaviors. But most often, we cast judgments about other people and never look within to see how that judgment is also true for ourselves. Feeling triggered by a friend? Make a list of judgments about her and see how they're also true for you.

10. Long distance: When a friend moves, the friendship will most likely be affected in some way. People tend to drift apart when they aren't a part of each other's day-to-day sphere. So create a commitment to connect regularly and arrange visits that work for both parties. The loss of a friend is also an invitation to grieve and feel those feelings of sadness and loss.

11. Neediness: This is when we demonstrate an unhealthy attachment to a friend and have unrealistic expectations of them. When the friend doesn't comply in giving their attention or time, we get triggered and angry and may start to find faults and cast judgments toward them. Neediness can also be viewed as codependency. This behavior stems from seeking validation, approval, acceptance, security, and control outside oneself. As mentioned under "Insecurities," you'll want to work on finding and giving this approval to yourself.

12. One-sidedness: A one-sided friendship is an uneven relationship in which one friend gives more energy to the relationship than the other. The person giving more might be the one who's always making the plans, the primary person to call and catch up, and the one who goes out of her way to make herself available. If you're the one giving more in a friendship, ask yourself why you continuously over-give. What part of you requires a one-sided friendship to over-give to? You might find that you're enabling and over-giving out of fear of being alone or being viewed in a certain way for having the friendship, or out of some other fear that's hiding beneath your over-giving behavior.

13. Personal gain: A woman may be in a friendship only to get something out of it. And there's nothing wrong with benefiting from our relationships. I go into more detail on this in a bit. But for now, let's look at reasons why women entertain relationships for personal gain only. I'd say the main reason women do this stems from believing that what we're seeking is outside ourselves, as discussed under "Insecurities." So, for example, a woman might be friends with someone she doesn't truly enjoy spending time with solely because she wants to be viewed by others as beautiful, popular, successful, spiritual, credible, or [insert insecurity here]. Other reasons may be to get ahead in her career, make more money, make new connections, gain opportunities, or even receive insider information. To avoid using others for personal gain in a disingenuous way, be up front and candid about your intentions, motives, and desires. State them clearly and ask for help. Most people can usually sense when there's something off in a relationship, so it's best to just be up front with others about your needs.

14. Too busy: So many of us are swamped with all that goes on in life! We're managing families, running organizations, starting/scaling businesses, working multiple jobs, launching campaigns, holding down 40-to-70-hour workweeks, managing our health, caring for elderly family members, and providing for our children in a million different ways. As a result, keeping up with friends sometimes just falls lower on the long list of priorities. So don't take it personally if you feel blown off by a friend. Instead, look within to see why you feel triggered by being blown off, share this with your friend, and then learn from what surfaces.

I'm pretty sure this list could go on, but for now we'll end it here. We know that we're complex beings, that our nature is multidimensional, and that our interactions with one another are therefore just as layered, intertwined, and multifaceted. We're all seeking to improve and deepen our connectivity with one another in some way, to be known, and to be understood. But if we can have the courage to know ourselves better and find acceptance for our imperfections, then can we understand and accept others for who they are as well.

Every time I bring up the topic of women, friendships, and our interactions with one another, more often than not, it's mutually agreed upon that women can be difficult to get along with—and that true friendships are very rare.

So if you're reading this book and thinking, *Damn, I don't have a close friend I can call up to drive me to the airport,* or *I don't have a best friend to celebrate my latest win with,* or *I don't feel deeply connected to the women in my life,* I want you to know that you aren't alone. So many women feel this exact same way.

According to Survey Center on American Life's May 2021 survey, only 59% of Americans have a best friend, which is a decrease from 75% in 1990.

Ladies, that leaves 41% of us flying solo most of the time. The survey also shares that an alarming 56% of American women aren't satisfied with their current friendships!

Whoa. That's really eye-opening!

So if anything I've said so far resonates with you in the slightest, it's because there are so many of us—approximately more than half of all women—who are struggling and unsatisfied in their relationships with other women.

CHAPTER 2

What's the Real Problem?

I've written this book specifically for conscious women who want to cultivate meaningful friendships with like-minded women who are also committed to a path of personal growth. There is immense value in having these types of relationships in your life because you thoroughly enjoy spending time with one another AND when conflicts arise, there is emotional maturity and understanding to not take things personally, but to support one another in grow-ing through your issues so they stop recycling in your life. It's a co-committed friendship revolving around deep trust, vulnerability, transparency, honesty, and growth so you both can become the best versions of who you are meant to be in this life.

A **true friendship**, also known as a conscious friendship, is one you enjoy giving your love and support to and is entertained for the purposes of growth and evolution in each person.

Let's read that again. And slow it down this time so it can really sink in.

A true friendship is one you enjoy giving your love and support to and is entertained for the purposes of growth and evolution in each person.

In a true friendship, nothing is needed in return as you give your love and support to your friend. This type of exchange feels different from other friendships. Simply by sharing your personal gifts of who you are and what you do best, your love, and support, you're expressing the highest version of yourself, which is not only beneficial to your friend but also to you in that you both get to experience an elevated version of who you truly are and the vibrational frequency that accompanies this higher self-expression.

But most importantly, a true friendship is entertained for the purposes of growth and evolution in each person. This is because as you engage regularly in the friendship, there is bound to be a reveal of your own triggers, projections, and relational disconnects that surface over time.

A true friend is not just a friend who gives unconditionally but is there to support you in moving through your own "stuff" so that you can evolve as a woman, as a better person, and this growth will be reflected in who you are for the rest of your life. You are co-commited learning partners just as much as you are friends.

Now that you understand these definitions more clearly, I need you to understand something else that's key:

You're not creating your reality just part of the time. You're creating your reality all of the time. You're responsible for your whole world and everyone in it because everyone is reflecting back to you who you are.

We all naturally have a habit of bypassing our problems because it's uncomfortable to face them. **This is the real problem.**

But once you understand that even the most painful experiences are created by us and for us, then you can begin taking 100% responsibility for all that you're creating and create something different instead of recycling your issues.

The problems that you face in your relationships with other women are your unconscious creations.

So, as you think about the list of the most common reasons we feel frustrated and disappointed in our relationships with other women, I want you to understand that these things are really just side effects of a much deeper issue. This unconscious behavior sabotages the true friendships you seek.

You might find it interesting that you're creating unconsciously, and you might also find it annoying in a sense. Because obviously, if you were aware of the unconscious things that you do to sabotage your success (in any category of your life), you wouldn't do them.

Just know this: what's present in your life right now is supposed to be there. If it wasn't supposed to be in your life, then it wouldn't be. Trust that what's present now is here for you to deal with now - and it's here for you at the perfect time to begin a practice of taking radical responsibility.

CHAPTER 3

Laundry Room Meltdown
and Super Cycles

When my daughter turned five, I planned a huge *Frozen*-themed birthday party for her. I'd attended a circus-themed birthday party for one of her preschooler friends the month before, which was like nothing I'd ever experienced in my life. They had life-size carnival rides, and not just one or two, but five or six rides. There was a freaking Ferris wheel, for crying out loud! That birthday party was amazing!

Now, I didn't have the budget for life-size carnival rides, but I felt inspired to go all out any way I could. I sat down and established my budget. From there I reserved a pavilion at my local park. I created an Excel spreadsheet (a Virgo tendency) to make a checklist of all of the things I would need. I enlisted family to bring dishes and help with decorations. I hired a professional Elsa to make a grand entrance. Ordered a custom-made *Frozen* dress for my birthday girl. And I sent out 30 or so handmade invitations using beautiful blue card stock complete with matching hand-tied bows.

I was excited, to say the least. But I also began to feel pretty stressed out as the RSVPs slowly trickled in. Only 12 of the 30-plus confirmed they'd be there. On top of feeling stressed, I began to feel disappointed by the low number of RSVPs, considering how much work I'd put into everything.

Unexpectedly, the day before the party, the weather report indicated that we would have tropical thunderstorms all weekend long. I live in Florida. It rains here often and usually clears up within an hour or two. I prayed this would be the case, as there was a no-refund policy on the pavilion and Elsa rentals, and it wasn't in my budget to pay twice. Also, the weather forecast isn't always reliable, so I decided to move forward with the party anyway.

I'm sure you can imagine what happened next. As the attendees also learned about the tropical storm that was underway, many of them canceled. And now there were only five kids planning to attend.

This realization took me into a downward spiral.

While attempting to do a last load of laundry to clean the white pants I'd planned to wear to the party, I suddenly and unexpectedly became overwhelmed with a flood of mixed emotions. I quietly shut the laundry room door for privacy from my family, then fell into a pile of laundry on the floor and cried. I felt ashamed, embarrassed, angry, and not good enough to have a successful birthday party for my daughter filled with her friends. And I'd put my heart and so much time into planning it.

And then out of nowhere, a flashback of my not-so-sweet-sixteen birthday party came into my mind, transporting me back in time. Only one friend, Brandy, was at my party—and that was because the party was at her house.

I'd planned that party the best I knew how—setting aside my favorite mixed CDs of 90s hits to play, picking out my favorite sparkly red dress to wear, and carefully sketching an accurate and detailed map to Brandy's house with a handwritten invitation that I made 30 photocopies of in my school's library. And I pushed myself out of my comfort zone to invite everyone I knew and liked at school.

A couple of my closer friends happened to have other plans the night of my party and unfortunately couldn't come. I was disappointed but decided not to reschedule. I assumed that out of all of the invites handed out, others would show. But when not a single person showed up, it was so embarrassing and left me feeling ashamed and unworthy of having friends show up to celebrate my sweet 16 birthday party. I left Brandy's house early that night, and as I walked home, I held in my tears and hid my shame so I wouldn't have to explain much when I got home early.

As soon as I got to my bedroom, I fell onto my messy bed, piled with laundry, and quietly sobbed so that my family wouldn't hear. The pain I felt in that moment hurt so bad that I couldn't endure it. So I pushed my shame away, wiped my tears, sat up, and told myself, "This is no big deal. I do have friends; they just couldn't come—that's all! And if anyone asks about how the party went, I'll just play it off. No one will ever know."

Looking back, it's actually a little comical when I think about it now. The party was to take place in Brandy's living room, which was very small—like, 15-people-were-too-many-people small. There was no entertainment, although we had a boom box with a three-CD disk changer of compiled hit songs. There were no decorations or party favors. Brandy's mom surprised us with a veggie-and-fruit platter, a bag of sour cream and onion chips, and a two-liter bottle of Sprite. Otherwise, there wouldn't have been any food. And there were zero RSVPs from the 30-something invitations I'd handed out. So yeah, I'd overlooked a few details in my planning. Just two girls, a couple snacks, and some 90s hits in a tiny living room. Oh, the humor of it all now! But man, what a huge disappointment that party was to me back then.

Nevertheless, when I came back from this mental flashback during my laundry room meltdown, I **intuitively knew** right then and there that if I didn't work on healing my worthiness issues with friendships, I would only pass down my unhealed trauma and feelings of unworthiness to my daughter. And I hated—let me repeat that—*I hated* how I was feeling in that moment so much that I couldn't imagine allowing that to happen.

In that moment, I promised myself that, when the time was right, I would prioritize healing my wounds surrounding my friendships. And I asked the Universe to guide me to healing them. This book is on the other side of and a part of that healing request from six years ago. It has been quite the journey.

I want to take a quick moment to point out the Super Cycle that was playing out in my laundry room meltdown. First, let's review what a Super Cycle is. A Super Cycle is also known as a cognitive-emotive loop (thought + emotion) that recycles stuck and old energy in your personal energy field as the result of a traumatic experience you haven't healed from. The Super Cycle unconsciously replays the trauma in your life in the form of real-life experiences over and over again with new people each time, or sometimes the same people. This repeating story plays out the same patterns of stuck emotions and thoughts in a similar situation each time.

In the book *A New Earth: Awakening to Your Life's Purpose,* spiritual teacher Eckhart Tolle refers to this stuck energy as the "pain body." Knowing that we have a pain body helps us understand that the energy of our traumas never leaves us, but stays with us in our personal energy fields until it's healed and transmuted. **Being aware of and present with the pain is what's required for the healing of it.**

When a strong emotion (energy in motion = e-motion) is repressed or suppressed, there's a possibility that the energy will result in a Super Cycle. Remember my walk home after leaving my party early and how I held in my feelings by suppressing them? And then how I sat on my messy bed of laundry when I got home and didn't allow myself to fully feel my feelings by cutting them off and giving myself a pep talk (repressing the emotions)? Well, emotions are meant to move through you all the way, not stop in the middle of their expression or be kept from being expressed at all. So the energy will manifest itself in some way. And therefore, it can become a Super Cycle, repeating the negative experiences in your life.

At first, you aren't aware of these negative patterns. They're blind spots and unconscious behaviors. But over time, as the negative pattern becomes increasingly painful, the discomfort wakes you up and you begin to recognize the Super Cycle playing itself out over and over again.

In my laundry room meltdown, I became aware of this Super Cycle as it was playing itself out, thanks to my flashback memory of my sweet 16 party fail. I also became aware of the similarities between both experiences: they occurred in piles of dirty laundry; they resulted in deeply painful feelings of shame, embarrassment, and not feeling good enough to have friends show up to an important birthday party; I'd invested a lot of my time and heart into planning them; and both were events I was really looking forward to.

In that moment, I chose to feel my feelings again, but only long enough to ask the Universe for help. The pain was intense, and I didn't have all the tools that I now share with you in this book. So I wasn't willing to fully face and feel it all in that moment. But a few years later, while I was at a leadership retreat, a separate but similar Super Cycle surfaced. And instead of it being in private, it happened in front of my peers. The exact same feelings of not being good enough and the shame I felt about them were laid out for all to witness. There was nowhere to hide, so in a triggered state I exploded into a cataclysmic public meltdown. Talk about an activated pain body!

Essentially, here's what happened. My conscious leadership cohort of about 25 people was meeting on Zoom due to COVID-19 restrictions. I was staying in a hotel at the beach to attend the retreat without distraction from work or family. The topic presented that day was emotive-cognitive loops (what I refer to as Super Cycles). While that moment is a little blurry, what I recall is one of the coaches spoke to me in a way that was deeply triggering for me. Because we were on the topic of emotive-cognitive loops, it was then pointed out that I was experiencing one in that very moment. Being made an example of is another trigger for me, and this situation ignited it. Others in the cohort made a few comments in response to the exchange, and before I knew it, my triggered state quickly turned cataclysmic.

In the moment of that meltdown and throughout that day, I did my absolute best to feel my feelings all the way. I pounded my fists, punched the bed, curled up into the smallest ball possible, and wailed as I released the emotional pain of not feeling good enough, which I'd been carrying around for most of my life. I took a nap on the beach that afternoon and even got up to go out into the water, where I screamed as loud as I could beneath the ocean so only the fish could hear. I was hyperaware of everything that day—I saw myself wanting to leave my hotel early as I began packing my bag in a state of flight. I hid from the retreat group and didn't rejoin them until the next day, I smoked a cigarette, drank a beer, ate a cheeseburger, and sat in a state of complete shock over what had just happened. My nervous system was spent.

The effects from that experience put me into a depression for a few months. But once that wore off, I'd rebirthed into a new woman—a woman with a strength and confidence I'd never felt before. I was done taking shit. I was done settling for less. I no longer had the capacity to entertain conversations, relationships, or friendships that weren't meeting me where I now was. I quit my corporate job of 12 years, cut ties with a few people, and flew solo for a few months with zero contact with any friends, focused only on me, my mental health, and my family.

And now when I look back on everything that happened, there's still some sadness that comes up, but overall, there's mostly appreciation—appreciation because the part of me that had once been haunted by not feeling good enough was transforming into a new confidence, a new knowing, and a new vibrational essence of who I am and what I will no longer accept. And I can see this new energy reflected back to me every time I host an event, throw a party, or call together a gathering of women. Instead of panic and anxiety like I used to feel, I now feel genuine joy, positive expectation, and trust.

What a beautiful gift that keeps on giving.

CHAPTER 4

The Leap

If you're reading this book, I trust there's a deeper reason. I don't believe in coincidences. You may have stumbled upon this book, but really, I believe there's an inner wisdom that guided you here. This wisdom within you seeks deeper connection with the women in your life and welcomes a breakthrough in your relationships that can be achieved only by doing the work of taking radical responsibility.

So right now, I'm asking you directly. Are you willing to take a leap of radical responsibility? Are you willing to look more closely at how **you're creating** the relationships you have with other women? Are you willing to do the uncomfortable work that comes with this practice, which will lead you to a path of rich connectedness, deep trust, and true *frientimacy*, with conscious and fruitful friendships that will enrich your life?

CHAPTER 5

What Is Radical Responsibility? And What Is It Not?

I f there's one thing I want you to take away from this book, it's the understanding of what radical responsibility is and what it is not.

Radical responsibility is exactly as it sounds: it's radical. It's radical because as a society, we're taught to look outside ourselves. When something doesn't go as planned and there's tension, pain, or discomfort, most people point outside themselves by blaming others for what went wrong.

The definition of radical responsibility comes from spiritual teachers Gay and Katie Hendricks, the best-selling authors of many books. My two favorites are *Conscious Loving: The Journey to Co-Commitment* and *The Big Leap: Conquer Your Hidden Fear and Take Life to the Next Level.*

I learned of this definition in my studies with The Conscious Leadership Group, as it's the first commitment of *The 15 Commitments of Conscious Leadership: A New Paradigm for Sustainable Success*—another favorite book of mine!

The definition is stated from two different points of view—from above the line and from below the line. In summary, above the line is where we aim to be. It's when we act from a place of presence, curiosity, trust, and openness. But below the line is how we're actually wired to respond. It's from below the line that we take most of our actions from a state of threat, righteousness, reactivity, scarcity, and fear and get stuck in the Drama Triangle.

Radical Responsibility Defined by The Conscious Leadership Group:

Above the line: I commit to taking full responsibility for the circumstances of my life and for my physical, emotional, mental, and spiritual well-being. I commit to supporting others to take full responsibility for their lives.

Below the line: I commit to *blaming* others and myself for what is wrong in the world. I commit to being a victim, villain, or a hero and taking more or less than 100% responsibility.

How Does Taking Radical Responsibility Actually Work?

Science tells us that our brains are hardwired to automatically scan our environment to identify threats. This survival tactic once served our cavewoman ancestors by helping them survive harsh living conditions and physical attacks by wild animals.

In modern times, however, the threats we face are rarely to our physical lives. These days, the most common threats we face are to our egos. Threats to our ego can feel very real and scary, or they can be cleverly disguised as a mild judgment.

Regardless, because our brains are constantly perceiving people and experiences as threats, it's up to us to recognize when this is happening and shift out of this fear-based thinking by acting consciously. Taking radical responsibility is one way to do this.

When you take radical responsibility, a shift from a state of threat to a state of trust occurs. Call it an energetic shift, a mindset shift, or a new state of being. Whatever you want to call it is up to you. But it's in this elevated state where we solve our most complex issues, discover win-for-all solutions, and enjoy new perspectives and opportunities with ease and joy.

CHAPTER 6

Steps in Taking
Radical Responsibility

Taking radical responsibility in our relationships with other women is going to play out differently for everyone, since we're all dealing with different situations. But essentially, the steps are the same and will be composed of the following:

1. Acknowledge your unconscious commitment.
2. Accept yourself for where you're at and the disconnection you've created from a triggered state.
3. Take your full 100% responsibility for creating the issue—not more than 100% and not less than 100%.
4. End blame and criticism of yourself and others.
5. Get curious about how this is here for your learning.
6. Assess your willingness.

Okay, let's jump into each of the steps in more depth.

Step 1. Acknowledge your unconscious commitment

Acknowledging the disconnection you're experiencing with other women is the first step in taking radical responsibility because it brings your awareness to the problem at hand and your role in creating it.

The dysfunctional, disconnected, or unsatisfying relationships you have with other women is what you're *unconsciously* committed to creating. As Jim Dethmer, from the Conscious Leadership Group, says, "You can always tell what a person is committed to by taking a look at the results in their life."

It feels good to acknowledge our manifestation wins. But it's even more powerful to **acknowledge and own the things you're** *unconsciously* **committed to creating** so that you can create an intentional life that reaches far beyond manifesting front-row parking spots. By acknowledging your unwanted creations and the role you play in creating them, you reclaim your power as a conscious creator of your reality.

Step 2. Accept yourself for being triggered

Once you've acknowledged your unconscious commitment, can you now look within yourself with true acceptance for having created the issue? Can you accept yourself for being scared? Can you accept yourself for creating the issue from a scared, threatened, and triggered state?

When you can accept yourself for being right where you are in the now moment—someone who created something because they were scared in a triggered state—this acceptance is powerful enough to shift your issue altogether.

Self-acceptance plays such an important role here. It's a defining moment in whether you'll be able to honestly take full responsibility for your unconscious commitment.

Step 3. Take your full 100% responsibility

When you tune into your unconscious commitment, ask yourself what 100% responsibility looks like for you. It's important to not take more than 100% or less than 100%. Just your 100%. Then, take the steps to fulfill that responsibility.

Also, I want to point out that if you're ever feeling confused about how to take radical responsibility, that's generally a sign that a part of you is unwilling to do so.

Step 4. End blame and criticism toward yourself and others

Blaming is the opposite of taking radical responsibility. Blame and criticism are rooted in fear—whether it's directed toward yourself or toward another woman. When we blame, it's because we're afraid of something. However, we don't always recognize our fears in the moments of blame because they're disguised as judgments and criticisms. Instead of blaming, conscious women end blame and take 100% responsibility for seeing not *if* they created the problem at hand, but *how* they created it.

Step 5. Get curious about how this is here for your learning

Even when you can't see any fault of your own (just like no one can ever smell their own bad breath), being curious about how you created this issue in the first place or how you keep recycling the same issues over and over again will help you see yourself more clearly.

So ask yourself:

"What this is here to teach me?"

"How is this for me?"

"What part of me keeps this issue going?"

Step 6. Assess your willingness

There are going to be times when you decide to take radical responsibility, but, because of a deeper subconscious unwillingness around your issue, that decision and intention won't be enough to succeed. And that's where the work of exploring your unwillingness comes into play.

The following is a list of Willingness Questions developed by the Conscious Leadership Group. They're designed to help people shift their issues from below the line to above the line.

Bring an issue with another woman to mind, then ask yourself the following questions to see if you're willing to fully shift your issue with her.

1. Am I willing to take 100% responsibility (not more or less) for this issue?
2. Am I willing to stop blaming and criticizing others and myself?
3. Am I willing to let go of being right?
4. Am I willing to get more interested in learning than defending my ego?
5. Am I willing to feel all of my authentic feelings (fear, anger, sadness, joy, sexual feelings)?
6. Am I willing to allow others to have all of their own feelings?
7. Am I willing to reveal to others all of my withholds?
8. Am I willing to speak unarguably?
9. Am I willing to listen consciously to others?
10. Am I willing to stop all gossip about this issue?
11. Am I willing to clear up all past issues with all relevant parties?
12. Am I willing to clean up all broken agreements related to this issue?

After scanning these questions, take note of which ones stand out and *lean into them*. Explore any unwillingness by welcoming it and accepting the part of you that's unwilling.

CHAPTER 7

Practicing
Emotional Intelligence

Sometimes our fears are legit, and other times they're just made-up stories based on past experiences or what we've seen happening in similar scenarios. They can also be what we're making up about what could happen.

But the truth is that your core emotions (fear, anger, sadness, joy, and sexuality/creativity) communicate information about yourself and your unique situations. And when you have the courage to confront your feelings and feel them authentically all the way through to completion, they bear gifts of wisdom that are deeply meaningful and beneficial for you.

The practice of feeling your feelings authentically is known as practicing emotional intelligence, which I'll refer to as EQ from here on out.

We all have the ability to practice EQ. In fact, it's actually our natural state. As children, we do this automatically. When a baby is sad, angry, or happy, you know it because they allow their feelings to come through. As adults, we suppress and repress our emotions every day and rarely give ourselves space to actually feel them completely.

And regularly feeling our emotions is a complete game changer for us women.

Practicing EQ will speed you up energetically as you move stagnant energy on a regular basis. As a side effect, it will raise your vibrational frequency. And it will cut through illusions in your life so that your truth and your path surface and become illuminated.

Hellooooo, manifestations that have been on back order!

I could probably write a whole book on the manifesting qualities that we access when we practice EQ regularly, and I just might one day. But for now, let's stay focused and just know that it's probably one of the most important tools I'm sharing in this book.

All feelings that come to mind when thinking of a relationship you struggle with are equally important to face and feel. Anger, sadness, joy, sexuality (aka creativity), and fear are our five core emotions, which all of our other emotions stem from. When we don't feel one, we affect our ability to feel them all. So you can't experience more joy without feeling your sadness, sexual, or angry feelings too.

Your emotions are energy in motion (think of the word *emotion* broken down as *e-motion* = energy in motion), and your feelings are meant to be felt (think of the word *feelings* broken down as *feel-ings*).

Steps for Practicing EQ

As taught by The Conscious Leadership Group

Step 1. Define the core emotion you're feeling (sad, scared, angry, joyful, sexual).

Step 2. Locate the sensation in your body. Bring your attention to the sensation and describe its precise nature as accurately as possible. Use verbs, like *twisting, popping, tightening, swirling*, or *flowing*.

Step 3. Breathe. Take a few gentle, full breaths, breathing as deeply as possible into your belly.

Step 4. Allow, accept, and appreciate the sensation. Ask yourself these questions: "Can I allow these sensations to be here? Can I accept these sensations as they are? Can I appreciate these sensations just as they are?"

Step 5. Match your experience with your expression. Use moving, breathing, and vocalizing (sounds without words) to match the sensation in and on your body. Ask the questions: "If the sensation could make a sound, what would it be? If the sensation could move, how would it do that?"

Step 6. Get the wisdom of the emotion.

- **Anger:** What is not or no longer of service? What isn't aligned? What needs to be changed or destroyed so something better can be put in place?
- **Sadness:** What needs to be let go of, said goodbye to, or moved on from? What person, dream, vision, belief, or opportunity needs to be released?
- **Fear:** What wants to become known? What wants to be faced? What do you need to wake up to? What wants to be learned?
- **Joy:** What wants to be celebrated? What needs to be appreciated? What wants to be laughed at?
- **Sexual:** What wants to be birthed or created? What attraction needs to be acknowledged?

CHAPTER 8

Why Most People Don't Take Radical Responsibility

You'll find that most people in general don't practice radical responsibility. Let's look at why.

On a macro scale, humanity is slowly waking up. Our parents, friends, family, teachers, the media, and global leaders are spiritually asleep in most cases.

Leonardo da Vinci said, "I awoke only to find that the rest of the world was still asleep." Well, this is what he meant. Leonardo was spiritually awake to the secrets of the mind, the heart, and the essence of our truth as spiritual beings having a human experience.

It is said that right now, more than ever before, we are in a mass spiritual awakening. People all over the planet are waking up to deeper truths within themselves. However, everyone is at their own level of this self-awareness, which is what's required for one to take radical responsibility. If there's no awareness of the self and no regular practice to cultivate awareness of self (meditation, for example), then the ego runs the show and the true self doesn't play as much of a role in your life.

This isn't necessarily a bad thing. I can see how the ego is of service, and I have deep appreciation for it. I also know many spiritually asleep people who are good-hearted and who live a very nice life. But there's a whole infinite universe of miraculous experiences on the other side of the veil of the sleeping consciousness. And once that veil is lifted, there's no going back. You can't shrink back your evolutionary conscious expansion. You can only continue expanding it.

Now, a woman seeking to end negative cycles in her experiences with other women and create more true friendships must have some level of self-awareness. Once she can see how she's creating her own issues through the lens of self-awareness, those issues begin to unravel and dissolve.

We naturally do better when we know better. And most of the time, we can't see how we're creating our own problems. That is, until our issues become so painful that we're forced to stop in our tracks and go a level deeper. Then our pain becomes the gateway to our healing. As Rumi said, "The wound is the place where the light enters you."

So on a micro scale, those of us who have self-awareness and are on a path of personal development still fall into the trap of blaming others for our problems. Sometimes we just forget that we're the creators of our realities.

We're also flowing in and out of different levels of conscious awareness all the time. It's a practice that takes practice! Not to mention, it can be hard work. Taking radical responsibility requires you to slow down and look at the issues that recycle in your life instead of bypassing them and numbing out with work, drugs, alcohol, sex, gambling, crap food, and, well, you get the point.

Radical responsibility takes time, energy, inner reflection, self-acceptance, vulnerability, and a lot of courage to face, feel, and accept the part of you that creates the problems.

CHAPTER 9

Challenges to Expect When Taking Radical Responsibility

As with anything new, we get better as we keep practicing. Taking radical responsibility is a practice, and the more you do it, the better you'll become at it. There are, however, some challenges to look out for. Knowing what these challenges are and what to expect will help you move through them.

Fear

I think one of the biggest challenges in taking radical responsibility is facing our own fears around the problems we have in our friendships with other women.

One helpful exercise is simply writing down your fears. This gives your fears a place to live outside your head. Sometimes they feel very real, and other times you start to see how ridiculous they are when you write them down. Either way, they can stop circulating in your mind.

Here are some of the common fears I see come up in friendships:

- Fear of losing a friend we've had for a very long time
- Fear of losing a relationship we deem beneficial (supportive to our career, offering opportunities, or influencing how others view us)
- Fear of being vulnerable, revealing our truth, being seen in an authentic way, and being judged for it
- Fear of hurting the other person's feelings
- Fear of feeling our own emotions
- Fear of loneliness
- Fear of the unknown and what this change will bring or mean for us
- Fear of being gossiped about
- Fear of being excluded from a group of mutual friends

Facing Your Fears Using EQ

Sometimes our fears are legit, and other times they're just made-up stories based on past experiences or what we've see happen in similar scenarios. They can also be disguised as anxious thoughts around what we're making up in our heads about what could happen.

But as discussed earlier about EQ, our emotions are communicating to us. Using EQ as a tool to face your fears as outlined above, or to feel any of your feelings that come up in your relationships with other women, will be a catalyst in your transformation to attract true friends in your life.

The challenge is that most women don't even know about this practice. It wasn't taught to us in school, and many of our parents didn't have this knowledge when raising us. Instead, society and our well-meaning parents raised us in a way that guides us away from going deeper into our feeling states. Some of the phrases we grew up hearing were: "Here, eat this. It will make you feel better." Or "Stop crying. Suck it up!" The good news is that you're learning about EQ now, and once you get some experience practicing it you'll have the opportunity to pass it down to your children and the people you love as a more effective way of managing emotions.

The other challenge is that feeling your feelings can bring about some discomfort in the moment. Feeling your anger, fear, or sadness doesn't feel good, which is why we often bypass feeling those emotions in the first place. Just know that emotions only last sixty to ninety seconds on average. So if you're willing to practice EQ, remember that the discomfort is temporary and the benefits far outweigh these temporary feelings of discomfort.

Clearing Conversations

In general, many people aren't skilled at having difficult conversations, so they avoid having them altogether.

Is this you?

While you may think you're doing yourself a favor by not revealing yourself to your friend, you could actually be doing more damage than you realize. Withholding thoughts, judgments, and feelings leads us to take an energetic step back in the relationship and project these thoughts and feelings onto the other person, which only sends the relationship into a downward spiral.

Writing out the situation and your feelings about it is a powerful process. Some people don't need to do this step, but if you think you'll go into the conversation feeling emotionally charged, say things that you might regret, then blame the other person for your experience, this is a must-have practice. After writing everything out, I suggest that you then make a short, bulleted list of things you'd like to communicate.

When taking radical responsibility in relationships I've struggled with, I've also found that true friends who are meant to be in my life respond differently than those I'm meant to move on from. It's as if clearing my feelings with them without blaming them for my negative experience reveals the truth and breaks through any illusions that I might've been holding on to.

Remember the saying, "The truth shall set you free"? This is that saying in action.

Eating Your Projections

One of the most powerful personal-development tools I've experienced is looking at my judgments of others, then seeing how this judgment I've projected onto someone else is also true for me.

It might not be an exact mirror of your behavior, but you can usually find the essence of the judgment within yourself if you look deep enough.

Remember, you don't see others as they are—you only see yourself as you are. Everyone in your life is a mirror of you and how you're showing up unconsciously.

Don't like how a friend is acting? Take a look at yourself to see how you can find their behavior within yourself.

Be gentle with yourself throughout these processes. There will be things you learn and unlearn every time you lean into one of these exercises. Don't beat yourself up for doing it "wrong." What's most important is that you intend to do better and create better friendships.

CHAPTER 10

The End of a Friendship and Taking Radical Responsibility

Several years ago I attended a Facebook marketing course at my local library. The room was packed, and I found myself sitting snugly between two people in the back of a computer room turned conference room. Midway through the program, I sparked a conversation with the woman sitting on my left. She had long brown hair, a friendly smile, and a funny sense of humor. She was smart and wore really nice shoes. She also showed me how to use the screen-filling emoji feature on my iPhone to send a funny text to a friend.

By the end of the workshop, I had made a new friend. We walked to our cars, talked a little longer, exchanged numbers, and made plans to connect in a couple of weeks.

That was the serendipitous start of my friendship with Melissa.

Months went by, and we found ourselves hanging out regularly. I loved hanging out with Mel. She was so funny, and I found myself always looking forward to our time together. Whether it was shopping, having dinner, exploring vegan festivals, or getting together for our birthdays, we always enjoyed ourselves.

Two amazing years of friendship went by in a flash. During this time, we learned about one another on a deeper level. After all, it was a judgment-free, safe space to share, which ultimately brought us closer together. At one point we even declared our "best friendship" to one another because, well, that's what it was.

One of the things Melissa shared with me was the real reason she'd moved to Florida. She'd been in a horrible marriage with a controlling and manipulative partner that ended in a nasty divorce. She'd basically lost everything. During and after the marriage, Melissa found refuge in drinking. But this refuge had taken a turn for the worse that ended up as alcohol addiction.

I had much empathy for Melissa and related to her in many ways. At one point in my life, I too had struggled with substance abuse, which led to my own move to Florida. And as a child, I experienced a similar divorce situation when my mother left my stepfather. With an open heart, I listened and showed Mel support in any way I could. None of her past mattered to me because I loved her and, well, the past is the past.

And then COVID-19 happened. In the beginning, the pandemic took a toll on every single person as the whole world was forced to shut down. And even though Melissa had established herself in a good place in her life, career, income, and sobriety, sadly, the pressure, stress, and fears that came with the lockdown sent her anxiety into overdrive and caused her to relapse.

The first time it happened, I was shocked. She seemed to be such a strong force, and she had come so far that I never saw it coming. Feeling a lot of fear and sadness for her relapse, I did what any friend would do: I went to her home to check on her, listened to her in her neurosis, cleaned her house, fed her dog, ordered takeout, encouraged her to eat, and meditated in her home to send her healing energy as she slept.

I called a mutual friend in her AA program to bring in more support. I had zero experience helping someone with alcohol addiction, and I found myself googling "how to help an alcoholic get sober" and "what to do when someone relapses." It was unfamiliar terrain that felt scary and intimidating. The weight of this experience consumed my life because it was all I could think about.

Shortly after the relapse, Melissa had a trip scheduled to visit her family out of state. The night before the flight, I encouraged her to stay at my house so I could drive her to the airport the next morning. Our mutual friend brought her to my home. When she arrived, I fed her a light vegan soup that would be easy on her stomach and gave her the spare bedroom so she could isolate herself as she sobered up from several days of binge drinking.

Several weeks after she returned to Florida, we picked back up as normal. Or at least we tried. When I attempted to speak to her about what had happened, she didn't want to talk about it, which was totally understandable.

But I couldn't ignore it. It had been scary! I also had so many things I wanted to tell her: how I was affected and how it impacted my family, and how I wanted to help. I also wanted to just clear the air. However, it was obvious that she wanted to move past it. So we did.

I felt angry, sad, and scared, but I held my feelings inside, hoping to move beyond them. I made up a story in my mind that she wasn't in the right mindset to discuss what had happened and was still feeling a lot of fear, shame, anger, sadness, and judgment toward herself.

(Note my judgment of Melissa here: "She wasn't in the right mindset to discuss what happened." We'll come back to this in a minute.)

When we hold things inside and don't clear our feelings, it costs us on an energetic level. Think of holding a beach ball under water. This takes a lot of energy.

That's what's happening when you don't clear your feelings with others. The energy you use to hold down the beach ball (suppressed feelings) would be better used to manifest your desires.

When you start regularly clearing your feelings, you'll see how quickly you feel better and how fast things start to move in your world. You'll also come to realize what not clearing your feelings is costing you. Knowing that you're missing out on something that you deeply want will become a powerful motivation for doing this work.

Note that I hadn't cleared my feelings with Melissa. And it wasn't long before we found ourselves in an argument.

After 10 minutes of shopping in a boutique health food store one day, out of nowhere Melissa indicated that she wanted to go to the car. "I'm going to go to the car so that no one breaks the windows open," she said.

"Ummm … okay!" I responded hesitantly, trying to keep the worry in my voice undetectable. In my head, though, I was thinking, *What the actual hell is she talking about? It's in the middle of the day! We're in a normal and safe part of town! What a random thing to say! She doesn't make any sense. She's not in her right mind ever since her relapse. I want to talk to her about this, but it's not safe to share my feelings with her. Ugh, I feel so scared to share my feelings with her! Why can't she just be open to talking?*

Here you can observe all of the unsaid judgments forming in my head: "Melissa doesn't make sense. She's not in her right mind. It's not safe to share my feelings with her. She's not open to talking."

On the drive home, using emotionally charged words (thanks to everything I'd been holding inside) I finally blurted out, "Melissa, you aren't making any sense! No one is going to bust out my windows. Why would you even say such a thing? It's a beautiful, sunny day out. We're in a safe part of town!"

"Ro, people bust out windows all the time when they see pets in cars! It's always happening on the news."

For context, Melissa's dog, Daisy, had been in my parked car with the windows cracked. It wasn't a hot day.

I hadn't felt concerned about Daisy being in the car because we'd taken measures to make her comfortable. I felt there was nothing to worry about. We could see the car from the store, as we were parked right in front. It wasn't hot at all, but we'd left the windows cracked to bring in a breeze.

Remember, the ego's job is to keep us alive. It does that by being right. And it collects data in our experiences as evidence to prove how right it is. In my case, to prove itself right, my ego discredited Melissa's concern about Daisy. Although the dog in the car was Melissa's concern, her initial statement about wanting to leave didn't include that. This confused me and made me want to validate my earlier judgment of her not being in her right mind.

So I replied, "Bad things happen on the news all the time. But I don't live my life worrying about every little thing that could happen. Obviously, if there's a reason to worry, then I'll be smart about it. But I'm not going to just worry about every little thing! What an unpleasant life that would be!"

Notice how I discredited the new information about Melissa's worry being related to her dog.

Some more words were exchanged as we ping-ponged back and forth in argument. We ended the conversation with so much tension and charged emotions that our hands were shaking and we glared in opposite directions to avoid eye contact.

Weeks went by, and I reached out to talk to Melissa about what had happened. Again, I found that she wasn't emotionally available to speak with me about our argument. She brushed it under the rug as if it had never happened.

She relapsed again, and this time I wasn't as involved as I'd been before. I knew she'd be okay and that she just needed to get through it. I wasn't going to make this a codependent relationship. So I gave her space and checked in on her. This time she assured me she'd gone back to AA and got a sponsor for support.

I felt hopeful. But our relationship wasn't what it had been. And without the ability to speak to her about things that bothered me, I felt unresolved and unsure of our friendship.

We finally decided to get together for a night out on the town. We texted about our plans in the weeks before. She'd recently moved, and I was excited to see her new place.

Upon arrival, I was disappointed to find out that she'd relapsed yet again. She answered the door in pajamas, reeking of alcohol, and speaking in a way that sounded unstable—almost as if she'd taken on another personality. It didn't feel like her. It *wasn't* her. The fun and funny friend I'd once loved was no longer shining through.

I helped her get ready and made her go out anyway, thinking maybe it would be good for her to get out of the house. After all, maybe I could get her to eat something. She ate a little bit of a meal and continued drinking. Her small talk with the men at the bar was very forward and presumptuous, which wasn't like the Melissa I knew. I was embarrassed by how she was acting, so I cut our night short and made it back to her place just after 11:00 p.m.

I slept on the couch and woke up to find her drinking vodka out of the freezer.

I left early the next morning and headed home.

Eventually, I decided to make one last attempt via email to address all the fallings-out we'd had and what she was going through with her relapses.

Her response was unwelcoming, angry, defensive, and just downright mean. It was clear she had no interest in resolving matters.

That was the last time we spoke.

Before and after sending the email, my work involved listing all of the judgments I made about her and seeing how they were true for myself (also known as eating your judgments/projections), then sitting with my emotions and feeling them through all the way to completion as best as I could.

Clearing my emotions with Melissa allowed me to release my pent-up feelings, stories, and judgments, and take my responsibility for my part in creating the disconnection.

Based on her response, it was clear that this wasn't the type of friendship I wanted to entertain.

Examples of How I Ate My Judgments/Projections

Melissa is addicted to alcohol. *I'm addicted to sugar and diets.*

Melissa is mentally unstable. *I'm mentally unstable. I actually have to meditate daily to manage my emotions, and I see a therapist from time to time to help me see situations more clearly. I'm also an overthinker and can easily obsess over details that don't really matter and create unnecessary conflict.*

Melissa needs help getting sober. *I need help with my sugar and diet addictions, especially when it comes to staying accountable with what I've committed to.*

Melissa is emotionally unavailable. *I'm emotionally unavailable and need to feel my feelings and express them fully. I overanalyze and use my intellectual problem-solving instead of going into my body and feeling my emotions fully.*

Melissa worries over made-up things, like my windows getting busted out because of her dog being in the car. *I worry about made-up things when I make up arguments in my head that haven't happened but that I can see happening.*

Taking Radical Responsibility—Doing the Work

My Unconscious Commitment: I'm unconsciously committed to attracting a friendship with someone who isn't mentally stable, who's struggling with addiction, and who's not emotionally available.

Acceptance: Can I accept myself for being right where I am? Yes. Can I accept attracting this person into my life? Yes. Can I accept the part of me that struggles with addiction to sugar? Yes. I'm doing the work and learning to love myself just the way I am the best way I know how. Can I accept the part of me that's mentally unstable? Yes. I accept my mental instability. I make up a story that without my daily meditation practice, I wouldn't be in a good mental place and would be a much angrier and sadder person. And I accept that. Can I accept the part of me that's not emotionally available? Yes. I see the part of myself that likes to hide from emotional vulnerability with others, and that makes a lot of sense to me. And I can see the version of myself before I had the tools of EQ, a time when Melissa and I were closest, and how I held in most of my feelings instead of sharing them. And I can accept the loss of our friendship once I started becoming more vulnerable with her.

Taking 100% Responsibility: Am I willing to take 100% responsibility for creating this issue? Yes. I can see how I created the entire disconnection and how I attracted a friend like Melissa, and how that led to this outcome.

Ending Blame and Criticism: Am I willing to end blame and criticism toward Melissa? Yes. And also toward myself? Yes. I don't see anyone at fault here. Melissa is a beautiful human who is multifaceted and was having an experience, as was I. There are many stories I can make up about why she relapsed and why I was a part of it. I also see myself as having an experience that was very eye-opening for me and is helping me heal my own addiction to food. There's no reason to blame or criticize either of us. We were just two women experiencing one another. We're both beautiful and healing in our own ways. We're both going about life and having different experiences that resemble one another but manifest differently. We're both equally exquisite, kind, deeply loving, funny, and beautiful, inside and out.

Getting Curious: Am I willing to see how this relationship with Melissa is here for my learning? Yes. Very much so. And I'm deeply grateful for it.

Assessing My Willingness: I've reviewed all of the willingness questions and can honestly say that I answered yes to them. I can see how I attracted this friendship with Melissa, how I created the disconnection with her, and how it was for my learning.

CHAPTER 11

The Reward of This Practice

A year ago, I signed up for a Kundalini retreat in central Florida with Guru Jagat. The program's focus was feminine friendships, and I could feel that it was exactly what my soul was seeking.

My good friend and Kundalini sister Paula excitedly signed up to attend the retreat with me. Since we're both local to South Florida, we looked forward to a fun-filled road trip to attend the retreat.

However, a month before the retreat, we received shocking news: Guru Jagat had passed away from cardiac arrest caused by a pulmonary embolism following surgery on her ankle.

Whoa. No one saw that coming. It was a horrible and unexpected tragedy. I'm still deeply saddened that we lost such a powerful spiritual teacher at such a young age in this sudden and unexpected way. (R.I.P. Guru Jagat.)

Guru Jagat's organization, RaMa Institute for Applied Yogic Science, decided to keep the retreat as scheduled but change its location from central Florida to California, closer to the RaMa headquarters in Venice.

With this change, Paula could no longer attend. But this retreat was a gift for my fortieth birthday, and I could feel the pull of my intuition telling me to go. So I went!

The retreat was now being held in the Big Bear Mountains of California, a two-hour drive from Los Angeles International Airport. This was a big concern for me because I have narcolepsy, which means I rarely drive long distances. Fortunately, RaMa gifted attendees a $200 travel credit, which covered my flight, and created a participant sign-up sheet for rideshares to and from the retreat. I was fortunate to be matched up with Sarah, who was willing to drive us. I saved her number in my phone as "Rideshare Sarah" and set out to meet her in California.

Leading up to the retreat, I began to feel depressed about the current state of my friendships. Sure, I had plenty of acquaintances, but I didn't have a close friend who could take me to the airport and who would go out with me to celebrate my birthday. Even though travel is one of my favorite things, I wasn't feeling excited about my trip. I was lonely, sad, and depressed. I missed Melissa and was reflecting on the close friends I'd outgrown. I was at a new phase in my life and had no one to really talk to about it.

I decided that traveling alone was the perfect opportunity to do what one of my mentors had taught me: exaggerate my feelings of loneliness and welcome them fully while being present in my body. So that's what I did. I welcomed my loneliness and embodied my depression.

I pouted. I put on a resting bitch face the entire afternoon of my first day in L.A. I kept all communications short. No small talk. I found a hotel on the beach near the Santa Monica Pier, then I lay in bed curled up feeling as sad, depressed, and lonely as I could for as long as I could. I went out to dinner and overate as a sad person would, then took a long walk on the pier. I embraced the loneliness as I watched the dark Pacific Ocean waves crash into the pier.

"What wants to be let go of? What wants to be grieved?" I reflected on these questions. I turned in early, allowing myself to rest. The next morning, I woke early to meditate on the beach. I watched the surfers catch waves and thought of all of the relationships I'd left behind in my recent departure from corporate work. I thought of Melissa and wondered what she was up to. I thought of how perfect it was that Paula couldn't come with me because I really needed this time to myself.

I continued my practice of embodying my depression, allowing myself to grieve and sit in my sadness. I felt gray, like the sky.

Yes, I was wallowing in my sadness. But it was on purpose. When emotions aren't felt fully, they end up staying in the body, and their energy comes out sideways and manifests in ways that are unpleasing. Chronic illness is an example of this. The more we can be in the present moment with our emotions, the more we're able to fully experience life and access a state of aliveness.

Later that day I met up with Rideshare Sarah, and we instantly hit it off. On our way into the mountains, we stopped for Mexican food, which is a favorite food for both of us. We immediately found common ground, since we're both daily Kundalini meditators and artists. It was a perfect rideshare match that I felt grateful for.

During the retreat, we shared a cabin and found ourselves naturally gravitating toward one another. When it was over, Sarah gave me a ride back to the city so I could catch my flight home. We parted ways only to catch up soon again via text. Since then, she has visited me in Florida, and we have become great friends—even accepting a thousand-day meditation challenge!

I know this friendship was made possible only because I allowed myself to go into the depths of my sadness and depression and do the work of feeling everything in my body. Once we get the lesson that our emotions are communicating to us, they've done their job and we're freed up energetically to entertain what comes into our lives next.

In addition to my connection with Sarah, there are about six other newer friendships that have developed since then. These friendships feel genuine, the conversations we have are meaningful, and the time we spend together is fun, enlightening and supportive. When challenges arise, transparency and vulnerability are at the forefront. These true friendships are enriching and deeply fulfilling. I love them, and I'm grateful to see my own transformation reflected back to me through these new women in my life.

CHAPTER 12

Taking Radical Responsibility Leads to Better Relationships

The journey of taking radical responsibility for the relationships you want isn't always an easy path. But if you feel called to do this personal-growth work, I promise that you won't regret it. It's game-changing in a potent and powerful way that undoubtedly leads to personal transformation and healthier relationships with yourself and others.

I'm sure you've heard before that your "vibe attracts your tribe" or that "in order to be successful you need to surround yourself with successful people." I agree with all of that. At the same time, I'm here to tell you that if you want true friendships with deeply loving, intuitive, authentic, successful, and conscious women who are doing the deeper work to heal and evolve, then you must become that woman yourself.

Your friendships with other women are a mirror of who you are. And the way to evolve into this improved version of yourself is by taking radical responsibility for what you're already creating in your life.

In my first attempt to take radical responsibility for my uneven friendship with Amanda, I stumbled through the radical responsibility process for the first time. It was a scary conversation to have, and I was terrified to take that step. Not only was it difficult to let go of the longest friendship I'd ever had—which was something I valued so much—but it was even more challenging to be so vulnerable and share so authentically all the things I'd held deep inside for so long. And then on top of that, I did my best to release blame toward her and see the unevenness of our relationship as an experience to appreciate instead of being angry about it.

So, while it was an uncomfortable experience, it was necessary for my growth and evolution toward developing better friendships and ending the cycle of over-giving. Deep down, I was seeking friendships that could offer a more meaningful experience. I was seeking conscious friendship.

Because our brains are wired to default into fear-based thinking, it's perfectly normal for us to seek outside ourselves to gain something from our relationships with others. This is why we often show up in friendships seeking something from the other person and find ourselves asking, "What am I gaining from this experience or person?" or "How does this relationship benefit me?"

This is perfectly normal and natural, and there's nothing wrong with asking yourself these questions. In fact, it's important that you do, because these questions lead to clarity about the types of friends you want to surround yourself with.

However, a conscious, true friendship is the opposite. **A conscious friendship is one in which you enjoy giving your gifts**, and there's a balanced relay between both ships. Get it? *Relay-tion-ship.* There's a mutual back-and-forth relay between ships.

Yes, think of ships on the ocean here. Two ships relaying back and forth to one another. When one stops sending messages to the other, that ends the relay-tion-ship.

And while there's nothing wrong with having friends you benefit from knowing, just note that these are not true friendships. These are acquaintances, community friends, work friends, etc. And we need those in our lives too!

But in a conscious, true friendship, there's nothing you need to get or gain from it. Although you could be gaining from it, this isn't the sole focus of the relationship. In giving your gifts to your true friends, you get to experience and enjoy the highest version of yourself, as do they. And this connection feels very different from a friendship in which one person, or both people, are trying to get/gain something from one another.

If you're wondering what your unique gifts are that you can give to the true friends in your life, consider this an invitation for self-exploration. Take a look at the things you're naturally gifted at and enjoy doing. Then, make a list in your phone and find ways to support your friends in these ways. Over the years I've seen this translated into insightful advice from a life coach, editing/review support for a book, décor and wall paint suggestions from an interior decorator, accountability for developing a new habit, website help and advice, the sharing of social media growth tips, artwork or handmade crafts as gifts, bringing a friend dinner during a busy/stressful time in their life, support when a friend starts a new business by sharing about it with others, making purchases from a friend's business, sharing a favorite meditation, showing up to a friend's speaking engagements/public events and bringing other friends along to create a supportive crowd, helping organize a party or big event, consciously listening to a friend who's going through a tough time, and overall just thinking of ways to support friends throughout life. Take the time to reflect on how you can support a friend, and then follow through. Or ask your friend what you can do to support them. Then follow through with no expectations of receiving anything in return.

CHAPTER 13

The True Friends Checklist

- There is mutual relay between both parties.
- You enjoy giving your gifts to this person. They accept your gifts, and the giving feels good to you.
- You don't seek to get anything out of the friendship other than the enjoyment of spending your time together and giving your gifts. The friendship could be beneficial, but that's not the main reason for having it.
- You can truly be yourself around this person. True friends don't care about how you dress, how clean your home is, or if you carry a high-end purse. If you find yourself worrying about these things to impress a friend, then this is a hint that this person isn't a true friend and you're seeking approval outside yourself.
- You have common interests, and both of you enjoy your time with one another.

- The friendship is fun and easy, and you look forward to spending time with your friend.
- When you feel triggered in the relationship, you feel safe enough to do the hard work of breaking your unhealthy relationship patterns and face your demons together.
- The friendship is energizing and feels good to you. You look forward to spending time with your friend and when they've departed, you continue to feel energized.

CHAPTER 14

Taking Radical Responsibility Transforms Your Feelings from – to +

There's something to be said for doing this type of personal-growth work. In my more than 12 years of consciousness studies, I've never experienced anything quite like it.

At first, taking responsibility for what's happening in your relationships with other women can seem confusing and intimidating. On one hand, you might be wondering, *How the hell am I creating these results in my relationships?* Or perhaps you're in the midst of a familiar cycle that you're looking to change once and for all but don't know how to move forward in a new way. When you go to take your next steps, they might feel terrifying. You may experience procrastination and a build-up of mixed emotions, such as fear, anger, and sadness.

It's perfectly natural to feel this way. This work makes you vulnerable and uncomfortable. Regardless of where you're at, **it's key to acknowledge and accept yourself for being right where you are and having all the feelings you have. Allow yourself to be with all your feelings in the present moment, for as long as you are able to. Don't skip over this.**

Once you've taken the time to get fully present and allow your feelings to surface, and you've spent some time feeling them fully, you'll be in a much better position to have that difficult conversation, express your truth, and say what needs to be said without blame.

Get past these uncomfortable parts, and I promise, the payoffs are immeasurable.

For one, you build mega courage muscles and mad communication skills doing this work. Having difficult conversations and saying what you're afraid to say is one of the most character-building exercises I know of. Think about it. The courage that it takes to face your fears, look at the parts of yourself that would rather stay tucked away, feel the feelings that come up, then share this with grace is profound work that will change you on a deep level.

Another positive outcome is that doing this work cuts through any illusions and puts you on the right course for you, which is better than being energetically stuck.

What do I mean by "cutting through the illusions"? When you've made up stories in your mind about the way things are or how you think they should be, doing this work exposes those illusions and reveals the truth. And once the truth is right in front of your face, you can't help but take the right course of action, even if that means moving on and leaving behind someone you love.

Sometimes we don't realize how much a relationship is actually costing us on an energetic level. The energy you spend worrying about a friend, a conversation, how someone is doing, or how they'll handle xyz is energy that you could otherwise spend on building a business, developing a new skill, landing a new dream job, or creating pretty much anything that your heart desires.

If you're not doing the work of taking radical responsibility, it's because you don't realize what not doing it is costing you. And once you get a taste? Well, let me just say there's no going back. You'll begin to move stagnant energy within you by taking radical responsibility. And that speeds up the Universe's creative flow that conspires to give you everything you desire.

The truth shall set you free, my friend.

CHAPTER 15

The Real-Life Benefits to You and Your Relationships with Other Women

Aside from significantly strengthening your communication skills, building your courage muscles, and developing your character as a conscious woman who's rising into her highest potential, new and better friendships with other women will come your way as a result of taking radical responsibility. And these new friends will mirror back to you the new version of you.

How about that! So as you improve yourself through this work, your friendships will also improve.

And the relationships that survive your radical responsibility process will improve. Those women will become closer friends. They'll be your true friends. And there will be a deeper trust, connection, and intimacy that you both will feel and enjoy.

What about the friendships that don't necessarily pass the test, so to speak? Well, they move on, and you learn valuable lessons that you'll carry into all of your future friendships.

As messy as this whole process can seem when you're in the thick of it, it truly is a beautiful unfolding that's changing the world one woman at a time. Even the friends who have moved on from your life will be affected in a positive way. You may never know exactly how, but you can trust that your personal-growth work creates a ripple effect in them too.

CHAPTER 16

How This Work Helps the World

This next section of the book is my favorite. I've given this topic a lot of thought over the years and have been moved to tears on so many occasions, I can't even count. When I think about the importance of the rise of the feminine and the rebalancing of masculine and feminine energy throughout the world, I can't help but envision a better world for us all.

Yeah, I know. It's deep. I'm deep. Welcome to my world!

But stick with me here. It's good.

I want to start by acknowledging that the timing of this book coming into the world isn't a coincidence. I believe that women's work of cultivating better relationships with other women is needed now more than ever because right now we're in a new astrological age: the Aquarian Age.

Approximately every 2,160 years, the sun's mathematical position moves into a new zodiac constellation. Astrologers agree that this change is happening right now and that with each new astrological age, humanity is affected in a big way. And by "big way," I'm referring to the rise and fall of civilizations as well as to the substantial changes in our cultural tendencies.

This is what we're going through right now as we move out of the Age of Pisces and into the Age of Aquarius. Below is a chart that shows these differences, many of which you've witnessed or experienced for yourself.

AGE OF PISCES	AGE OF AQUARIUS
Patriarchy	Feminism
Them vs. Us	We instead of Me
Hierarchical Governance	Horizontal Self-Governance
Religious Beliefs	Spiritual Awakening to Self
Blind Faith	Intuitive Self-Knowing
Needing an External Savior	Being Your Own Savior
Rigid Family Structure	Fluid Family Groups
Traditional Sexual Roles	Fluid Intimate Connections
Planetary Exploitation	Planetary Sustainability
Linear Thinking	Intuitive, Creative, Artistic, and Emotional Thinking
Male Dominated	Unity in Diversity

Looking back in U.S. history, we saw legislation changes that began the support of this shift starting in the mid-1800s and early 1900s with the women's suffrage movement. And throughout the 1900s and 2000s, we saw many new firsts for women.

Here's a short timeline of some of the more notable changes in the United States supporting the shift from the Age of Pisces to the Age of Aquarius. It's not all inclusive and supports no party affiliation.

1848 - Women's suffrage movement begins.

1916 - Jeannette Rankin becomes the first woman elected to U.S. Congress.

1920 - Women gain the right to vote.

1932 - Hattie Caraway is the first woman elected to serve in the U.S. Senate after first filling a vacancy caused by her husband's death in 1931.

1947 - Women can serve on juries.

1973 - Abortion becomes legal.

1974 - Women can take out a line of credit and own property in their own name without the consent of their husbands.

1981 - Sandra Day O'Connor is the first woman to serve on the Supreme Court.

1998 - Employers become liable in sexual harassment cases.

2005 - Condoleezza Rice becomes the first Black female secretary of state.

2008 - Hilary Clinton runs for president and is the first nominee of a major political party.

2010 - Women are provided birth control without copays and deductibles, giving them better access to affordable health care.

2013 - Women can participate in combat.

2015 - Same-sex marriages are made legal nationwide.

2021 - Kamala Harris becomes the first woman to serve as vice president of the United States of America.

At the time of writing this book (2022), according to the Center for American Women and Politics' website, women represent 27.3% of 535 seats in Congress, 31% of 310 seats of statewide elected executives, and 31% of 7,383 seats in state legislatures.

It's radical to think back to the times when women didn't have the liberties and freedoms we enjoy today in the United States. It's also sobering to know that not only do we have much work to still do, as represented in our current political numbers, but there are so many women in the world who don't get to experience these basic freedoms—women whose lives are suppressed by their communities, educational systems, cultural beliefs, religions, husbands, governments, and laws. All of this keeps them from knowing and experiencing our norm. These women are instead forced into motherhood, denied education, subjected to limited access to health care, and forced to live every day without a voice or choice. And let's not forget the sexual exploitation of women, from human trafficking of selling women, teenagers and young girls as sex slaves, all the way up to the #MeToo movement, which speaks to every single woman in the world.

And last, there's the pandemic of women worldwide who don't know that they're enough: good enough, smart enough, educated enough, rich enough, pretty enough, skinny enough, fill-in-the-blank enough. The list of lies goes on and on and runs deep in so many of our subconscious programs, holding all of us back.

So you get my point. Ladies, we have some work to do on ourselves and in our relationships with other women. And this work will contribute to a collective healing for us all.

So, welcome to the dawn of a new age for humanity—the undercurrent for this work. We each have a responsibility to fulfill, and it's up to you to answer the call within. I believe you were drawn to this book because you're part of a much bigger picture—the bigger picture that bands women together and calls on us to set aside our differences, stop taking things so personally, take responsibility for the realities we're creating, evolve through healing and self-awareness, and use our energy to create something new in the world.

CHAPTER 17

You Have a Choice

Now you have a decision to make for yourself. You can keep waiting until later to do the work that will result in better friendships and more connectedness with the women in your life. You know, that someday when you'll have more time, more money, more energy. But isn't that what you've been doing up until now? You can take this information and say to yourself, "Wow, this book really helped me see my relationships with women more clearly. I'm inspired, and I really think I can do this now." But you already know what's down that path. It's not a new feeling. It's the same feeling you get every time you watch an inspirational YouTube video, listen to your favorite motivational speaker, or read another game-changing self-help book.

The other choice is to answer the inner calling that's guiding you to do the deeper work required for transforming—not just your relationships with women, but all of your relationships.

And then you can enjoy the rest of your life's journey nurturing the best friendships and most fulfilling relationships that life has to offer you. If you make this choice, you'll always have the tools and resources within to navigate challenges as they come up. You'll be able to deepen your relationship with your true, authentic self and show up in a way that's magnetic, graceful, fun, and expressive of your full aliveness and highest potential. This can be you. However, making this choice requires you to do something different than you've been doing.

CHAPTER 18

How I Can Help

Y ou can reach out and get help with anything that has come up for you as you read this book. Yes, I'm happy to help you. Really. It's what I do. It's what I love, and it's what I'm most passionate about. Not to mention, I'm pretty fun and easy to talk to!

So let me invite you to go to my online calendar right now to book a time to speak with me personally. I'll ask you some questions about what has drawn you to do this work, your vision, and your challenges. Whatever your biggest challenges are, I promise you, I've heard it before—and I'm actually really good at identifying the real problem and helping find a solution that will work. Breakthrough results are what I'm most proud of when it comes to helping women transform their lives.

So here's how it works. We'll get on the phone for 45 minutes or so, and I'll ask you enough questions to see if I can help make a simple, but powerful plan for guiding you to do the deeper and more profound radical responsibility work that's outlined in this book. This work will help you transform from the inside out in a way that reflects real change in all of your relationships and interactions with others. Whether your goal is to stop a repeating pattern of self-sabotage once and for all, let go of friendships that are no longer serving you, create a breakthrough in your life, or attract the loving, fun, and authentic conscious women who will stick around for the long haul, I can help you.

To paraphrase my favorite Rumi quote, whatever you're seeking, it's also seeking you. And I can help you achieve results in a way that works for you.

How Much Does It Cost?

The session is 100% free.

Who Is This Really For?

One of the most important things to know in business is who you *can't* help. I certainly can't help everyone, nor do I have any interest in trying to do so. I'm often asked why I work only with women. The answer is simple: it's my calling. I know in my heart that I was put on this Earth to help women step into their highest potential and evolve through the challenges they face.

And on an energetic level, there's nothing more expensive than working with the wrong people, so it's got to be a perfect fit for the both of us. In order for me to help you in this session, here are the qualifiers:

You've got to be serious about creating a real shift in your life and have a real desire to experience something different from the results you've been creating.

I need you to have a whole-body yes to doing this work, show up on time, and follow through with any commitments you make to yourself.

You've got to have a level of self-awareness and know that you're the creator of your reality.

You've got to be familiar with energy work in general. You don't need to be an expert, but I need you to know what it is.

You've got to have some type of daily practice—preferably one that involves daily meditation—or be serious about starting one and sticking to it. The work we do together thrives when you're in a clear mental state that's achieved through a daily meditation practice.

You've got to know about the magic in you and in the world, and have experienced your multidimensional nature as a woman who has the ability to create anything her heart desires—a woman who has nothing but the best of intentions for herself, others, and the world, and who is ready to create more of what she desires in her life.

What's the Catch?

Again, the session is free. Why do I do them? Simple. It's how I fill my business with clients. During the call, we'll get to know each other and whether your desires and my expertise are a match. We'll also see if our personal styles mesh or not. On my end, if I feel three things during our call, I'll most likely invite you to work with me personally in my Highest Potential program, a self-mastery program for conscious women.

Here are the three things:

1.) I need to like you (and vice versa).

2.) I need to know 100% that what I offer will help solve your problem and get you what you want.

3.) I need to be very confident that if you do exactly what I tell you, the results are well within your reach.

If all three elements are in place, I'll share more about how the program works and how you can be a part of it. If we get to the offer, you'll either decide that it's a perfect fit for you, or you won't.

I leave that up to you. But whatever you decide, we'll part as friends.

To book your call with me now, go to

www.RochondaFerrelli.com/TrueFriends

You'll pick a time and answer a few short questions so I can get to know you better before we speak. It will take you about five minutes.

Once we're together, I promise that our time will be highly focused on your vision and challenges. I'll do my very best to paint a picture of success specific to your needs and situation, and provide what I can to support your next steps. I value my time, so I'll respect yours as well and make the session as helpful as I can for you.

Whether you decide to take me up on my offer or not, I sincerely hope this book did what I promised it would do—help you see yourself and your relationships with women through a new lens so that this perspective can support your personal-growth journey to discover and enjoy more fulfilling friendships.

Feel free to share your thoughts with me at ro.ferrelli@gmail.com. In closing, thank you for joining me here and for sharing this book with a friend who also needs to hear this message.

About the Author

Rochonda Ferrelli is an entrepreneur and creative. She is the CEO of Highest Awakened Potential, a coaching company designed to support Conscious Entrepreneurs in developing their leadership skills and growing their businesses beyond six figures. But before coaching entrepreneurs, she previously spent 15 years as a Life Coach to multisensory women helping them uplevel their lives, relationships, careers, and incomes. And she wrote this best selling book, True Friends, to support all women in their personal evolution.

Rochonda is also a professional artist and the creator behind the Magnetic Geodes by Rochonda brand and art mentorship programs.

You can visit her websites:

www.RochondaFerrelli.com

www.MagneticGeodes.com

And if you stop by RochondaFerrelli.com, make sure to sign up for her monthly newsletter where she shares wisdom and resources to help entrepreneurs shift into their highest awakened potential and create sustainable success in their businesses.

Free Bonuses & Gifts from the Author

Included with this book are 2 training videos accompanied with pdf downloads to support your true friends journey. One on Practicing Emotional Intelligence for Beginners and the other is on Clearing Conversations for Beginners.

Access them for free at

www.RochondaFerrelli.com/TrueFriends